George Weah
Taking on 170-Year
Challenges of Liberia

Moses Kulo

PAGE PUBLISHING, INC.
New York, NY

First originally published by Page Publishing, Inc. 2018

ISBN 978-1-64298-237-4 (Paperback)
ISBN 978-1-64298-238-1 (Digital)

Printed in the United States of America

This book is dedicated to the people
of Liberia and their future.

Contents

List of Figures

Introduction

The primary purpose of the book is to create awareness about the leading factors and causes that are responsible for Liberia's challenges now facing President Geoge Weah. Liberia was the first free, independent country on the continent of Africa in 1847. Liberia is financially supported and politically guided by the great United States of America for many decades. In recent years, other countries around the world have joined the United States to improve the quality of life of the Liberian people. Also, Liberia has natural resources such as iron ore, timber, diamonds, gold, rubber, and a productive land suitable for subsistence or industrial farming. Historically, the population of Liberia has not reached 5 million. The highest population recorded was about 4.73 million (United Nations, 2017)

Since1847, despite the international communities' supports and the natural resources, majority of the people in Liberia are living in poverty. In the early 1990s, thousands of Liberians died in the civil war; the economy, infrastructures, and institutions were destroyed while hundreds of thousands of Liberians went into exile to save their lives. This book identifies and explores some of the past and present governments' policies and practices that contributed to the destructions of lives, our democracy, and other institutions that resulted in no development in Liberia.

The book is not intended to open the wounds of the Liberian people but to enlighten their minds to make wise decisions that would improve the lives of all Liberians beyond the 2017 General and Presidental Elections. Great nations had experienced challenges in the past, but none would allow the history to repeat itself. Liberia's future depends on agenda, policies, and practices of Liberia's future leaders. Therefore, this book contains recommendations that will help our leaders develop and implement policies and practices that will result in development in Liberia.

Economic and Political Journeys

Many scholars will agree that Liberia began an independent nation in 1847 with promising economic and political futures than other countries in Africa. Liberia has no colonial master like many African countries. The founding fathers of Liberia were Africans who returned from the United States as free people supported by American Colonization Society (ACS). Roberts Finley of New Jersey, USA, established ACS in 1816 purposely to help the migration of free African-Americans to Africa.

Liberia's relationship with the United United benefited the Liberian people. Liberia naturally became a democratic nation. English became an official language, and many Liberians converted to Christianity. The ACS and the United States government provided the needed fund to build Liberia's economy in the 1800s. Also, ACS guided the development of the Liberian political institution. The governing body of ACS led Liberia from 1822–1847 when it turned over the leadership of Libera to the free African-Americans known as Americo-Liberians. Liberia immediately declared independence from ACS and became a sovereign nation in Africa.

In 1869, True Whig Party was founded as a political party by the Americo-Liberians. Unfortunately, the leaders of this new party formed an autocratic government and became, laying the foundation for a self-centered political ideology that destroyed Liberia's social, economic, and political institutions for many decades. Ideology is a particular set of political practices, ethical ideals, principles, doctrines, or a collection of ideas of any social class. The True Whig Party focused on promoting and protecting the interests of Americo-Liberians and ignored social, economic, infrastructural, and human development in Liberia.

Sadly, in the late 1800s and early 1900s Liberians were divided into two groups namely indigenous and Americo-Liberians. The government of Liberia did nothing to unite the Liberian people. Even the government engaged in practices that encouraged and promoted disunity of the two groups. For example, the indigenous people were not allowed to participate in the political, decision-making process of the country. However, few Americo-Liberians supported the integration of the Liberian people. Some of the Americo-Liberians encouraged and supported indigenous citizens to improve their social and economic statuses. For example, some private Americo-Liberians financially supported the native population to go to school through nongovernmental organizations.

Lessons Learned

In the past two hundred years, no other ideological institution in the Western Hemisphere besides democratic system has survived the human, economic, social, and political challenges of our time. Let us make it clear, many countries in the West claimed to be democratic when in practice, they are not. Liberia is one of those countries. One of the pillars of Western democracy, civilization, equality, economic progress, and moral well-being is making or following fair laws.

The Liberian government, especially under True Whig Party, missed an opportunity to develop and support policies that could reduce illiteracy, improve the community, economic development, strengthen the nation's infrastructure, and bring the people together. The so-called elite class (Americo-Liberians) only focused on enhancing its members' economic and political security. Historically, no government or social class in the Western world is capable of protecting itself without the support of its people. The Liberian government's lack of support from the majority of the citizens resulted in the violent destruction of the government under True Whig Party in 1980.

Military Action, Not a Solution

The military overthrew the True Whig Party government April 12, 1980. It's impossible to defend the records of any Liberian leader before 1980. There was a definite need for change. However, the Liberian people did not intend to replace autocratic leadership with a de facto administration. The military government's decision to murder the officials of True Whig Party by a firing squad in 1980 was not what Liberians anticipated as the solution to our nation's challenges. There is no time to rewrite our history, but we need to recognize that punishing our fellow Liberians who committed economic and political crimes against our people by unlawful means is not in the best interest of our nation. Illegal punishment is a crime and should not be used in a democratic country.

Disrespecting the rules of laws and the Constitution of Liberia led to the downfall of the military government that replaced the True Whig Party. Those seeking political offices must understand that nearly all past and present Liberian leaders who deployed iron-hand leaderships in nearly two centuries had failed to prevail. The people of the Republic of Liberia show no sign of embracing an undemocratic institution in the previous two decades, now, and in the future.

Solutions to Liberia's Challenges

S trauss (2016) identifies the most challenging problems facing Africa as lack of economic growth, unemployment, poor education, poverty, ill health, violence, and corruption in governments. These are the issues that make it harder for development to take place in Liberia. These problems are not unknown to Liberians and their leaders. The real question is why these challenges have not been solved? Many leaders, private citizens, international communities, and governments had tried and failed because those in government in Liberia had no real desire, motivation, and determination to solve those problems. For nearly two hundred years, Liberian leaders favor the country's well-known saying: "Monkey works baboon draws." At this moment, many Liberians and our international friends will agree with Lagrade (2015) that this is not the right time for "monkey works baboon draws" practice. Liberian leaders must abandon strategies that will continue to destroy the fabric of our society. It's misleading to say Liberia will achieve a middle-class income status by 2030 while years after years the Liberian leaders continue to make and implement monkey-work, baboon-draw policy. For example, let's look at the Liberian lawmakers' salaries based on 2015–2016 National Budget.

Most of our nation's budget is allocated for the salaries of those who prepared the budget. In contrast, the ordinary civil servants' wages including teachers, doctors, police officers, and nurses are below the poverty level in Liberia. Those individuals, despite their critical roles and responsibilities in society, are living in poverty.

The higher salary explains why Liberia looks like a nation in the eighteenth century. Almost all of the resources are being used to pay salaries of the few top government officials. The colossal wages mean nothing left to improve education, health care, infrastructures, and quality of life in Liberia. Therefore, the first reasonable step for putting Liberia on the right path to greatness is to appropriately allocate the nation's resources to benefit the entire population. It's necessary to reduce the salaries and eliminate most of the benefits of the top government officials in Liberia.

	ALLOCATIONS FOR LIBERIAN LEGISLATURE (IN US$) NATIONAL BUDGET 2015–2016				
	HOUSE OF REPRESENTATIVES			HOUSE OF SENATE	
	Speaker	Deputy Speaker	Each Member	Pro Tempore	Each Member
Basic Salary	65210	64740	34956	105227	34482
General Allowance	257412	132065	81736	247325	107622
Special Allowance	72000	60000	30000	78000	30000
Transp. Reimb. Allowance			38400		38100
Foreign Travel (tickets)	21065	14400	1700	19710	2493
Foreign Travel (food/hotel)	35340	32461	9991	32617	5242
Foreign Travel (incidental)	42318	14400	14000	2415	18
Domestic Travel	12000	12600	6000	7800	20128
Telecom/Internet/Post	12000	28000	13793	20158	16957
Water and Sewage			1056		
Residential property lease	24000	24000	12000	20149	15656
Fuel Vehicle	117960	100000	42371	74850	45499
Fuel Generator	47256	41000	2465	33408	2586
Repair and Maint. Civil			2852		1724
Repairs Vehicles	40000	36000	19832		1724
Repair Machinery			19225		1034
Cleaning Materials			985		517
Stationery	15000	6000	1702	10000	2586
Printing, Binding, Publications	12006	5000	354	2404	334
Newspapers, books, mag.	6000	2100	78		172

Other Specialized Materials	12000	85000	19938	217648	35896
Scholarships—local	15000	10000	2000	6028	2000
Entertain., Repres., Gifts	18000	15000		12943	34
Workshops, conferences, etc.			70		26
Operational Expenses	15000	15000	704	22073	690
Grand Total	444945	440961	209516	482203	193416

Figure 1. Public Source: Liberian Lawmaker Watch, Institute for Research and Democratic Development

Democracy is the world's best political apparatus for more than two hundred years. A democratic form of government has stood the test of time in the last two centuries than any other kind of government in the world. Democracy is superior because its principles rely on the will of the majority rather than a single person or few individuals in society. For example, despite political challenges in the United States, the country remains the world's greatest economic, political, and super military power. The source of the United States superiority is the democracy. The people, political parties, and government of the United States remain committed to a democratic institution regardless of their differences and political affiliation.

Democracy is not just electing leaders for governance, but also for making fair laws and making sure the laws protect every citizen. The laws must equally apply to every person regardless of position, social status, religion, political affiliation, and nationality. The people of the United States, especially politicians and officials in government always favor appropriate application of the laws. Appropriately interpreting and applying the laws make the United States a genuinely democratic nation in the world.

The people of Liberia, particularly the politicians and officials in the government, will benefit from the model of American democracy. The greatest challenge in Liberia is that most of the people in government do not practice what they learned. Many of the individuals in government studied in the United States. Those people understand the principles of democracy but choose to serve their interests rather than follow democratic principles. So the second solution that may change the course of history in Liberia is that all Liberians including private citizens, politicians, and government's officials must be prepared to make the necessary sacrifices by following the democratic principles.

Figure 2. Executive Mansion in Monrovia, 2009

President Ellen Johnson Sirleaf's Agenda

E very leader who occupied the Executive Mansion and led Liberia in the past 170 years had an agenda that focused on many of the problems in the country. Unfortunately, no leader was successful in addressing a single critical issue mainly due to at least one or more of the following reasons: the leader's poor judgment, incompetent staff, corruption, and inability to follow established protocols by the people in each administration. Many international experts on Africa thought Ellen Johnson Sirleaf, the first female democratically elected president in Africa, could be the first to provide solutions to the nation's social, economic, education, infrastructure, and healthcare challenges. Those experts were wrong. President Johnson holds a master's degree in public administration from Harvard University. She worked at the World Bank in Washington DC. Later, she returned to Liberia and served as deputy minister of finance and minister of finance in the Tolbert's administration from 1977 to 1980. President Johnson made the worst strategic blunder in history after the civil war when she approved exorbitant salaries and benefits for ministers, directors, legislators, and other top employees in her government.

After the civil war, mostly Liberian government depends on donors to provide essential services in the country since the war destroyed many sources of national revenues. Limited revenues forced her to divert the funds received from donors for national development to pay salaries. Also, her government was paralyzed by corruption. The most important responsibility of the president is to make sure that the key government officials honestly and fairly perform their official duties in the interest of the state and people. Many of her government officials accepted bribes and made decisions, not in the interest of the state and people. For example, the Sable Mining Company bribed some of her officials with $950,000 (US dollars) for a favorable contract. Lack of drastic penalties for public officials who committed crimes contributed to rampant corruption in Africa (Okekeocha, 2013). Limited fund and corruption in government ended President Sirleaf's dream of laying the foundation to turn Liberia into a middle-class nation by 2030.

Liberia's future leaders need to learn a valuable lesson here. Corruption is the threat to prosperity in Liberia. Your determination to bring social and economic well-being, rebuild Liberia's infrastructure, education, healthcare system, and agricultural industry will fail if you surround yourself with dishonest and corrupt officials. Leading in Liberia is a daunting task that requires more robust and aggressive approach to stop corruption, which is the real threat any modern president faces.

Figure 3. Ellen Johnson Sirleaf, the 23rd President of Liberia

Mother of Democracy

Even though President Ellen Johnson Sirleaf did not accomplish most of what she wanted to do as president, she will be remembered in history as a mother of democracy in Liberia. In the last few months of her presidency that ended on January 22, 2018, she fought brilliantly against her party to ensure a peaceful transition of power. The vice president Joseph Boakai, a presidential candidate and his supporters, repeatedly attacked President Sirleaf for not using her power to bend the rules in favor of the vice president like many Liberian leaders in the past. Many claimed she was supporting the main opposition presidential candidate, Senator George Weah of the Coalition for Democratic Change (CDC). The Youth Wings of the Unity Party introduced a plan to kick President Sirleaf out of the party. She refused to give in to their pressure. There was no evidence that she was not supporting UP. According to Malayea and Harmon (2016), President Sirleaf told her party (425 delegates) in Bong County that she supported Baokai to continue the party's development agenda after she left office in 2018. She set an example for our future leaders. Democracy is the bedrock of any modern society. In a democratic nation, the people's right to choose their leader through the ballot box under the constitution must be respected by the present and future leaders.

Geoge Weah's Remarkable Journey

M r. Geoge Weah was not born with a silver spoon in his mouth. He was born on October 1, 1966, in Clara Town, one of Monrovia poorest neighborhoods. Weah entered the world with exceptional, unique skills in soccer. After a remarkable display of talents playing soccer for Mighty Barrolle, Invincible Eleven, and the great Lone Star of Liberia from 1985 to 1987, he took his skills across the Atlantic Ocean to Europe in 1988. Weah dominated most of the games he played on every team in Europe. Presently, he holds the world's record as the only soccer player in history to score 193 goals in 411 professional appearances. Also, he won several awards and recognition for his accomplishments on the field.

Figure 4. The world's best soccer player

George Weah won his first African Player of the Year award in 1989. At his best in Europe, he won Ballon d'Or with AC Mian in 1995 and became the European and World Player of the Year.

Leaders Are Born Not Made

The world-renowned researchers in the United States, Europe, and other countries indicated that leaders are born and not made (Hyacinth, 2014). These scholars implied that leadership is a matter of personality. It's the traits or personal characteristics of a person that influence his or her followers. George Weah's natural talents and leadership skills confirmed and demonstrated what researchers found about leaders.

After his retirement from soccer, he redeployed his talent as a goodwill ambassador for the United Nations to end the civil war in Liberia in the 1990s. He was successful and became a living legend of his people. Weah wanted to do more for Liberia. So he formed a political party known as Congress for Democratic Change (CDC) and unsuccessfully contested the 2005 election as a presidential candidate. His political adversaries claimed that he was not experienced and not educated enough to become a president. He returned to school and earned a master's degree in public administration in 2013 from DeVry University, an accredited American university. He returned to politics and became a Montserrado County senator on January 14, 2015, to silence his critics.

Figure 5. Senator George Weah, Republic of Liberia

He now has the education and experience. Also, what his political opponents failed to realize was his charisma or strength of character that made him likable. Many Liberians called him the king of our generation. So when he decided to run for the 2017 presidential election, his party became an unstoppable political powerhouse in Liberia. Weah advanced to the runoff of the 2017 presidential election to face the sitting vice president Joseph Boakai. On December 26, 2017, Weah won the presidency after nearly three months of legal battle between the Liberty Party (LP), Unity Party (UP), and National Election Commision (NEC), intended to delay or destroy the electoral process underway in the country.

Can George Weah Accomplish
What Others Failed to Do?

Winning the presidency in Liberia is like clearing the mine-field to begin the real battle. Liberia is in the deplorable state. The country still depends on foreign aid. The government still uses about 80 percent of the national revenues to pay top employees. There is no sign of development and employment opportunity. Education, healthcare, infrastructure, and social services are collapsing. Corruption remains rampant in the government. President Weah faces a tall order in his new presidency. The Liberian people and the international community are on edge and were wondering whether Weah would be able to deal with the problems facing the country.

This book provides useful ideas to assist any modern leader of Liberia. The key to overcoming these tremendous challenges is to surround yourself with people who will put Liberia first. One of the British prime ministers, Winston Churchill, suggested a unique approach to dealing with problems in a fragmented society for ever-lasting peace, stability, and economic progress. He said, "If we open a quarrel between the past and the present, we shall find that we have lost the future." Weah is carefully trying to protect the future by doing what Churchill suggested. The president-elect Weah uses his acceptance speech to call on all politicians and Liberians at home and abroad to continue the rebuilding process of Liberia where the outgoing president Ellen Johnson Sirleaf left off. Weah is not just a skillful leader with charisma, but also someone who truly loves his country and people. With the cooperation of all the political parties and the people of Liberia, he will accomplish great things for our country. We all need to put our nation first regardless of political affiliation. President Weah is ready to work with every Liberian to deliver what our nation deserves.

Weah Wants to Improve the Economy

Immediately after the National Election Commission of Liberia declared Weah the winner of the 2017 presidential election, he told the world that Liberia was ready for business. He promised to protect the interest of local businesses and international investors to help improve the economy. The president-elect made unprecedented political maneuvering when he appealed to the man he defeated in the presidential election and the leaders of all political parties in the country to join him to work for the Liberian people. Also, he assured the Liberians and the international community that his administration would not tolerate corruption. The new president wanted to unite the country to focus on what kept our people in poverty for one hundred seventy years. Also, these pronouncements showed that Weah was ready to make a difference in the life of every Liberian.

References

Hyacinth, B. (2014). Are leaders born or made? A true story

Lagards, C. (2015). Liberia: Overcoming Challenges-Past, Present, and future, International Monetary Fund

Malayea, M. & Harmon, Q. (2016). Liberia: Ellen reaffirms support to VP Boakai, Daily Observer, Monrovia, Liberia

Okekeocha, Chinelo, "A Case Study of Corruption and Public Accountability in Nigeria" (2013). *Dissertations, Theses and Capstone Projects*. 566. https://digitalcommons.kennesaw.edu/etd/566

Strauss, G. (2016). Six challenges facing Africa, democratic Sub-Sharan Africa, Trade & Economics

United Nations, (2017). World population review Liberia-population

About the Author

Moses Kulo was born to Mr. and Mrs. Kai Kulo, subsistent farmers in the south-eastern part of Liberia. After completing his high school in Liberia, he moved to the United States for further studies. He earned a doctorate in education (EdD) from Walden University, based in Minnesota, in the United States of America. Also, he is a graduate of Prairie View A&M University in Texas, USA, with a master's degree in sociology (MA) and bachelor of business administration (BBA) with a concentration in finance.

Dr. Kulo has twenty years of professional teaching experience with the Houston Independent School district, the seven-larger school district in the United States. He received several awards as an outstanding educator. He attended and presented at teacher professional developments.

After earning his doctorate in 2012, he decided to contribute to his community. He worked with his fellow Liberians to craft the Constitution of the Liberian Association of Greater Houston (LAGH). Later, Dr. Kulo joined the Congress for Democratic Change (CDC)-USA, trying to improve the lives of the people in Liberia. He served as vice chairman/international of the Global Fundraising Committee (GFC) created to support the presidential campaign of the Liberian president George Weah. Also, he served as senior researcher and adviser to the Media and Communications Team of the Coalition for Democratic Change (CDC) that helped elected Weah as president of Liberia.

CPSIA information can be obtained
at www.ICGtesting.com
Printed in the USA
LVHW050736030322
712397LV00004B/622

9 781642 982374